STUDIES IN SOCIOLOGY

This series, prepared under the auspices of the British Sociological
Association, is designed to provide short but comprehensive and
scholarly treatments of key problem-areas in sociology. The books
do not offer summary accounts of the current state of research in
various fields, but seek rather to analyse matters which are the
subject of controversy or debate. The series is designed to cover a
broad range of topics, falling into three categories: (1) abstract
problems of social theory and social philosophy; (2) interpretative
questions posed by the writings of leading social theorists; (3) issues
in empirical sociology. In addition, the series will carry translations
of important writings in sociology which have not previously been
available in English. Each book makes a substantive contribution
to its particular topic, while at the same time giving the reader an
indication of the main problems at issue; each carries an annotated
bibliography, comprising a critical survey of relevant further
literature.

ANTHONY GIDDENS

University of Cambridge

STUDIES IN SOCIOLOGY

General Editor: ANTHONY GIDDENS
Editorial Advisers: T. B. BOTTOMORE, DAVID LOCKWOOD
and ERNEST GELLNER

Published

MARXIST SOCIOLOGY
Tom Bottomore

POLITICS AND SOCIOLOGY IN THE THOUGHT OF MAX WEBER
Anthony Giddens

PROFESSIONS AND POWER
Terence J. Johnson

POWER: A RADICAL VIEW
Steven Lukes

CONSCIOUSNESS AND ACTION AMONG THE WESTERN WORKING CLASS
Michael Mann

Power : A Radical View

STEVEN LUKES

Fellow and Tutor in Sociology and Politics,
Balliol College, Oxford

palgrave

Published by
PALGRAVE
Houndmills, Basingstoke, Hampshire RG21 6XS and
175 Fifth Avenue, New York, N. Y. 10010
Companies and representatives throughout the world

PALGRAVE is the new global academic imprint of
St. Martin's Press LLC Scholarly and Reference Division and
Palgrave Publishers Ltd (formerly Macmillan Press Ltd).

ISBN 0–333–16672–8

This book is printed on paper suitable for recycling and made from fully managed and sustained forest sources.

A catalogue record for this book is available from the British Library.

18   17   16   15
05   04   03   02

Printed in China

For Sally

CONTENTS

PREFACE

This book began as a lecture to Pierre Birnbaum's students at the Sorbonne. It then became a seminar paper, delivered at the political sociology seminar which I helped to run at Oxford, along with R. W. Johnson, Roderick Martin and Frank Parkin. It then went through many revisions, in the light of discussions, notably at the Université de Montréal and McGill University in Montreal and the University of Massachusetts and the New University of Ulster at Coleraine, and of the probing arguments and criticisms of (among others) Brian Barry, John Gaventa (who is testing out some of its ideas in empirical research), Jerome Karabel, Jackie Lukes, José Maravall, Kenneth Newton, Bertell Ollman, Frank Parkin, Bob Rae, Joseph Raz, Frank Wright – and, above all, of Peter Bachrach, William Connolly and Alan Montefiore. I am especially indebted to Peter Bachrach. The public and private discussions we had during his stay in Oxford were unusual occasions in that opinions were changed, not just reinforced: they were for me exceptionally exciting and rewarding.

1. INTRODUCTION

THIS short book presents a conceptual analysis of power. In it I shall argue for a view of power (that is, a way of identifying it) which is radical in both the theoretical and political senses (and I take these senses in this context to be intimately related). The view I shall defend is, I shall suggest, ineradicably evaluative and 'essentially contested' [15][1] on the one hand; and empirically applicable on the other. I shall try to show why this view is superior to alternative views. I shall further defend its evaluative and contested character as no defect, and I shall argue that it is 'operational', that is, empirically useful in that hypotheses can be framed in terms of it that are in principle verifiable and falsifiable (despite currently canvassed arguments to the contrary). And I shall even give examples of such hypotheses – some of which I shall go so far as to claim to be true.

In the course of my argument, I shall touch on a number of issues – methodological, theoretical and political. Among the methodological issues are the limits of behaviourism, the role of values in explanation, and methodological individualism. Among the theoretical issues are questions about the limits or bias of pluralism, about false consciousness and about real interests. Among the political issues are the famous three key issue areas studied by Robert Dahl [12] in New Haven (urban redevelopment, public education and political nominations), poverty and race relations in Baltimore, and air pollution. These matters will not be discussed in their own right, but merely alluded to at rele-

[1] Contrast Parsons's lament that 'Unfortunately, the concept of power is not a settled one in the social sciences, either in political science or in sociology' ([26] p. 139). (References in square brackets refer to works listed in the Bibliography, pp. 59–64 below.)

vant points in the argument. That argument is, of its very nature, controversial. And indeed, that it is so is an essential part of my case.

The argument starts by considering a view of power and related concepts which has deep historical roots (notably in the thought of Max Weber) and achieved great influence among American political scientists in the 1960s through the work of Dahl and his fellow pluralists. That view was criticised as superficial and restrictive, and as leading to an unjustified celebration of American pluralism, which it portrayed as meeting the requirements of democracy, notably by Peter Bachrach and Morton S. Baratz in a famous and influential article, 'The Two Faces of Power' [2] and a second article [3], which were later incorporated (in modified form) in their book, *Power and Poverty* [4]. Their argument was in turn subjected to vigorous counter-attack by the pluralists, especially Nelson Polsby [30, 31], Raymond Wolfinger [37, 38] and Richard Merelman [20]; but it has also attracted some very interesting defences, such as that by Frederick Frey [14] and at least one extremely interesting empirical application, in Matthew Crenson's book *The Un-Politics of Air Pollution* [9]. My argument will be that the pluralists' view was indeed inadequate for the reasons Bachrach and Baratz advance, and that their view gets further, but that it in turn does not get far enough and is in need of radical toughening. My strategy will be to sketch three conceptual maps, which will, I hope, reveal the distinguishing features of these three views of power : that is, the view of the pluralists (which I shall call the one-dimensional view); the view of their critics (which I shall call the two-dimensional view); and a third view of power (which I shall call the three-dimensional view). I shall then discuss the respective strengths and weaknesses of these three views, and I shall try to show, with examples, that the third view allows one to give a deeper and more satisfactory analysis of power relations than either of the other two.

2. THE ONE-DIMENSIONAL VIEW

THIS is often called the 'pluralist' view of power, but that label is already misleading, since it is the aim of Dahl, Polsby, Wolfinger and others to demonstrate that power (as they identify it) is, in fact, distributed pluralistically in, for instance, New Haven and, more generally, in the United States' political system as a whole. To speak, as these writers do, of a 'pluralist view' of, or 'pluralist approach' to, power, or of a 'pluralist methodology', is to imply that the pluralists' conclusions are already built into their concepts, approach and method. I do not, in fact, think that this is so. I think that these are capable of generating non-pluralist conclusions in certain cases. It is, for instance, by using their view of power and their methodology for identifying it (so that the locus of power is determined by seeing who prevails in cases of decision-making where there is an observable conflict) that Robert McKenzie [19] concludes that power in the two main British political parties is pyramidal; and it is by using a different view and methodology that Samuel Beer [6] concludes that, in the case of the Labour party, it is not. The former view yields elitist conclusions when applied to elitist decision-making structures, and pluralist conclusions when applied to pluralist decision-making structures (and also, as I shall argue, pluralist conclusions when applied to structures which it identifies as pluralist, but other views of power do not). So, in attempting to characterise it, I shall identify its distinguishing features independently of the pluralist conclusions it has been used to reach.

In his early article, 'The Concept of Power', Dahl describes his 'intuitive idea of power' as 'something like this : A has power over B to the extent that he can get B to do something that B

11

would not otherwise do' ([10], in [7] p. 80). A little later in the same article he describes his 'intuitive view of the power relation' slightly differently: it seemed, he writes, 'to involve a successful attempt by A to get a to do something he would not otherwise do' ([7] p. 82). Note that the first statement refers to A's capacity ('. . . to the extent that he can get B to do something . . .'), while the second specifies a successful attempt – this, of course, being the difference between potential and actual power, between its possession and its exercise. It is the latter – the exercise of power – which is central to this view of power (in reaction to the so-called 'elitists' ' focus on power reputations). Dahl's central method in *Who Governs?* is to 'determine for each decision which participants had initiated alternatives that were finally adopted, had vetoed alternatives initiated by others, or had proposed alternatives that were turned down. These actions were then tabulated as individual "successes" or "defeats". The participants with the greatest proportion of successes out of the total number of successes were then considered to be the most influential' ([12] p. 336).[1] In short, as Polsby writes, 'In the pluralist approach . . . an attempt is made to study specific outcomes in order to determine who actually prevails in community decision-making' ([30] p. 113). The stress here is on the study of concrete, observable *behaviour*. The researcher, according to Polsby, 'should study actual behavior, either at first hand or by reconstructing behavior from documents, informants, newspapers, and other appropriate sources' (p. 121). Thus the pluralist methodology, in Merelman's words, 'studied actual behavior, stressed operational definitions, and turned up evidence. Most important, it seemed to produce reliable conclusions which met the canons of science' ([20] p. 451).

(It should be noted that among pluralists, 'power', 'influence', etc., tend to be used interchangably, on the assumption that there is a 'primitive notion that seems to lie behind *all* of these concepts' ([10], in [7] p. 80). *Who Governs?* speaks mainly of 'influence', while Polsby speaks mainly of 'power'.)

The focus on observable behaviour in identifying power involves the pluralists in studying *decision-making* as their central

[1] For a critical discussion of Dahl's use of his own concept of power, see Morriss [25].

12

task. Thus for Dahl power can be analysed only after 'careful examination of a series of concrete decisions' ([11] p. 466); and Polsby writes:

> one can conceive of 'power' – 'influence' and 'control' are serviceable synonyms – as the capacity of one actor to do something affecting another actor, which changes the probable pattern of specified future events. This can be envisaged most easily in a decision-making situation. ([30] pp. 3–4)

and he argues that identifying 'who prevails in decision-making' seems 'the best way to determine which individuals and groups have "more" power in social life, because direct conflict between actors presents a situation most closely approximating an experimental test of their capacities to affect outcomes' (p. 4). As this last quotation shows, it is assumed that the 'decisions' involve 'direct', i.e. actual and observable, *conflict*. Thus Dahl maintains that one can only strictly test the hypothesis of a ruling class if there are '. . . cases involving key political decisions in which the preferences of the hypothetical ruling elite run counter to those of any other likely group that might be suggested', and '. . . in such cases, the preferences of the elite regularly prevail' ([11] p. 466). The pluralists speak of the decisions being about *issues* in selected [key] 'issue-areas' – the assumption again being that such issues are controversial and involve actual conflict. As Dahl writes, it is 'a necessary though possibly not a sufficient condition that the key issue should involve actual disagreement in preferences among two or more groups' (p. 467).

So we have seen that the pluralists see their focus on behaviour in the making of decisions over key or important issues as involving actual, observable conflict. Note that this implication is not required by either Dahl's or Polsby's definition of power, which merely require that A can or does succeed in affecting what B does. And indeed in *Who Governs?* Dahl is quite sensitive to the operation of power or influence in the absence of conflict: indeed he even writes that a 'rough test of a person's overt or covert influence is the frequency with which he successfully initiates an important policy over the opposition of others, or vetoes policies initiated by others, or *initiates a policy where no opposition appears* [*sic*]' ([12] p. 66).[2] This, however, is just one among a number of examples of how the text of *Who Governs?* is more subtle and profound than the general conceptual and methodological pronouncements of its author and his colleagues;[3] it is in contradiction with their conceptual framework and their methodology. In other words, it represents an insight which this one-dimensional view of power is unable to exploit.

Conflict, according to that view, is assumed to be crucial in providing an experimental test of power attributions: without it the exercise of power will, it seems to be thought, fail to show up. What is the conflict between? The answer is: between preferences, that are assumed to be consciously made, exhibited in actions, and thus to be discovered by observing people's behaviour. Furthermore, the pluralists assume that *interests* are to be understood as policy preferences – so that a conflict of interests is equivalent to a conflict of preferences. They are opposed to any suggestion that interests might be unarticulated or unobservable, and above all, to the idea that people might actually be mistaken about, or unaware of, their own interests. As Polsby writes:

> rejecting this presumption of 'objectivity of interests', we may view instances of intraclass disagreement as intraclass conflict of interests, and interclass agreement as interclass harmony of interests. To maintain the opposite seems perverse. If information about the actual behavior of groups in the community is not considered relevant when it is different from the researcher's expectations, then it is impossible ever to disprove the empirical propositions of the stratification theory [which postulate class interests], and they will then have to be regarded as metaphysical rather than empirical statements. The presumption that the 'real' interests of a class can be assigned to them by an analyst allows the analyst to charge 'false class

[2] Emphasis mine (S.L.) This passage is acutely criticised in Morriss [25].

[3] Another example occurs on pp. 161–2 and p. 321, when Dahl points implicitly towards the process of nondecision-making, by writing of the power of members of the political stratum partly to determine whether a matter becomes a 'salient public issue' or not.

consciousness' when the class in question disagrees with the analyst. ([30] pp. 22–3)[4]

Thus I conclude that this first, one-dimensional, view of power involves a focus on *behaviour* in the making of *decisions* on *issues* over which there is an observable *conflict* of (subjective) *interests*, seen as express policy preferences, revealed by political participation.

[4] Compare Theodor Geiger's critique of Marx's imputation of 'true interests' to the proletariat which are independent of the wishes and goals of its members: here, writes Geiger, 'the proper analysis of the interest structure of social classes ends – religious mania alone speaks here' (*Die Klassengesellschaft im Schmelztiegel*, Cologne and Hagen, 1949, p. 133 cited and translated in Dahrendorf [13] p. 175).

3. THE TWO-DIMENSIONAL VIEW

IN their critique of this view, Bachrach and Baratz argue that it is restrictive and, in virtue of that fact, gives a misleadingly sanguine pluralist picture of American politics. Power, they claim, has two faces. The first face is that already considered, according to which 'power is totally embodied and fully reflected in "concrete decisions" or in activity bearing directly upon their making' ([4] p. 7). As they write :

> Of course power is exercised when A participates in the making of decisions that affect B. Power is also exercised when A devotes his energies to creating or reinforcing social and political values and institutional practices that limit the scope of the political process to public consideration of only those issues which are comparatively innocuous to A. To the extent that A succeeds in doing this, B is prevented, for all practical purposes, from bringing to the fore any issues that might in their resolution be seriously detrimental to A's set of preferences. (p. 7)

Their 'central point' is this : 'to the extent that a person or group – consciously or unconsciously – creates or reinforces barriers to the public airing of policy conflicts, that person or group has power' (p. 8), and they cite Schattschneider's famous and often-quoted words :

> All forms of political organisation have a bias in favour of the exploitation of some kinds of conflict and the suppression of others, because *organisation is the mobilisation of bias*. Some issues are organised into politics while others are organised out. ([34] p. 71)

The importance of Bachrach and Baratz's work is that they bring this crucially important idea of the 'mobilisation of bias' into the discussion of power. It is, in their words,

> a set of predominant values, beliefs, rituals, and institutional procedures ('rules of the game') that operate systematically and consistently to the benefit of certain persons and groups at the expense of others. Those who benefit are placed in a preferred position to defend and promote their vested interests. More often than not, the 'status quo defenders' are a minority or elite group within the population in question. Elitism, however, is neither foreordained nor omnipresent: as opponents of the war in Viet Nam can readily attest, the mobilisation of bias can and frequently does benefit a clear majority. ([4] pp. 43–4)

What, then, does this second, two-dimensional view of power amount to? What does its conceptual map look like? Answering this question poses a difficulty because Bachrach and Baratz use the term 'power' in two distinct senses. On the one hand, they use it in a general way to refer to all forms of successful control by A over B – that is, of A's securing B's compliance. Indeed, they develop a whole typology (which is of great interest) of forms of such control – forms which they see as types of power in either of its two faces. On the other hand, they label one of these types 'power' – namely, the securing of compliance through the threat of sanctions. In expounding their position, we can, however, easily eliminate this confusion by continuing to speak of the first sense as 'power', and by speaking of the second as 'coercion'.

Their typology of 'power', then, embraces coercion, influence, authority, force and manipulation. *Coercion*, as we have seen, exists where A secures B's compliance by the threat of deprivation where there is 'a conflict over values or course of action between A and B' (p. 24).[1] *Influence* exists where A, 'without resorting to either a tacit or an overt threat of severe deprivation,

---

[1] On coercion see Robert Nozick, 'Coercion', in *Philosophy, Politics and Society, Fourth Series*, ed. Peter Laslett, W. G. Runciman and Quentin Skinner (Oxford: Blackwell, 1972) pp. 101–35, and J. Roland Pennock and John W. Chapman (eds), *Coercion: Nomos XIV, Yearbook of the American Society for Political and Legal Philosophy* (Chicago/New York: Aldine-Atherton Inc., 1972).

17

causes [B] to change his course of action' (p. 30). In a situation involving *authority*, '*B* complies because he recognises that [*A*'s] command is reasonable in terms of his own values' – either because its content is legitimate and reasonable or because it has been arrived at through a legitimate and reasonable procedure (pp. 34, 37). In the case of *force*, *A* achieves his objectives in the face of *B*'s noncompliance by stripping him of the choice between compliance and noncompliance. And *manipulation* is, thus, an 'aspect' or sub-concept of force (and distinct from coercion, power, influence and authority), since here 'compliance is forthcoming in the absence of recognition on the complier's part either of the source or the exact nature of the demand upon him' (p. 28).

The central thrust of Bachrach and Baratz's critique of the pluralists' one-dimensional view of power is, up to a point, *antibehavioural*: that is, they claim that it 'unduly emphasises the importance of initiating, deciding, and vetoing' and, as a result, takes 'no account of the fact that power may be, and often is, exercised by confining the scope of decision-making to relatively "safe" issues' (p. 6). On the other hand, they do insist (at least in their book – in response to critics who maintained that if *B* fails to act because he anticipates *A*'s reaction, nothing has occurred and one has a 'non-event', incapable of empirical verification) that their so-called nondecisions which confine the scope of decision-making are themselves (observable) *decisions*. These, however, may not be overt or specific to a given issue or even consciously taken to exclude potential challengers, of whom the status quo defenders may well be unaware. Such unawareness 'does not mean, however, that the dominant group will refrain from making nondecisions that protect or promote their dominance. Simply supporting the established political process tends to have this effect' (p. 50).

A satisfactory analysis, then, of two-dimensional power involves examining both *decision-making* and *nondecision-making*. A decision is 'a choice among alternative modes of action' (p. 39); a nondecision is 'a decision that results in suppression or thwarting of a latent or manifest challenge to the values or interests of the decision-maker' (p. 44). Thus, nondecision-making is 'a means by which demands for change in the existing allocation of benefits and privileges in the community can be suffocated before they are even voiced; or kept covert; or killed before they gain access to the relevant decision-making arena; or, failing all these things, maimed or destroyed in the decision-implementing stage of the policy process' (p. 44).

In part, Bachrach and Baratz are, in effect, redefining the boundaries of what is to count as a political issue. For the pluralists those boundaries are set by the political system being observed, or rather by the elites within it : as Dahl writes, 'a political issue can hardly be said to exist unless and until it commands the attention of a significant segment of the political stratum' ([12] p. 92). The observer then picks out certain of these issues as obviously important or 'key' and analyses decision-making with respect to them. For Bachrach and Baratz, by contrast, it is crucially important to identify *potential issues* which nondecision-making prevents from being actual. In their view, therefore, 'important' or 'key' issues may be actual or, most probably, potential – a key issue being 'one that involves a genuine challenge to the resources of power or authority of those who currently dominate the process by which policy outputs in the system are determined', that is, 'a demand for enduring transformation in both the manner in which values are allocated in the polity . . . and the value allocation itself' ([4] pp. 47–8).

Despite this crucial difference with the pluralists, Bachrach and Baratz's analysis has one significant feature in common with theirs : namely, the stress on actual, observable *conflict*, overt or covert. Just as the pluralists hold that power in decision-making only shows up where there is conflict, Bachrach and Baratz assume the same to be true in cases of nondecision-making. Thus they write that if 'there is no conflict, overt or covert, the presumption must be that there is consensus on the prevailing allocation of values, in which case nondecision-making is impossible' (p. 49). In the absence of such conflict, they argue, 'there is no way accurately to judge whether the thrust of a decision really is to thwart or prevent serious consideration of a demand for change that is potentially threatening to the decision-maker' (p. 50). If 'there appears to be universal acquiescence in the status quo', then it will not be possible 'to determine empirically whether the consensus is genuine or instead has been enforced through nondecision-making' – and they rather quaintly add that 'analysis of this problem is beyond the reach of a political analyst and perhaps can only be fruitfully analysed by a philosopher' (p. 49).

This last remark seems to suggest that Bachrach and Baratz are unsure whether they mean that nondecision-making power cannot be exercised in the absence of observable conflict or that we could never know if it was. However that may be, the conflict they hold to be necessary is between the *interests* of those engaged in nondecision-making and the interests of those they exclude from a hearing within the political system. How are the latter interests to be identified? Bachrach and Baratz answer thus : the observer

> must determine if those persons and groups apparently disfavored by the mobilisation of bias have grievances, overt or covert . . . overt grievances are those that have already been expressed and have generated an issue within the political system, whereas covert ones are still *outside* the system.

The latter have 'not been recognised as "worthy" of public attention and controversy', but they are 'observable in their aborted form to the investigator' (p. 49). In other words, Bachrach and Baratz have a wider concept of 'interests' than the pluralists – though it remains a concept of subjective rather than objective interests. Whereas the pluralist considers as interests the policy preferences exhibited by the behaviour of all citizens who are assumed to be within the political system, Bachrach and Baratz also consider the preferences exhibited by the behaviour of those who are partly or wholly excluded from the political system, in the form of overt or covert grievances. In both cases the assumption is that the interests are consciously articulated and observable.

So I conclude that the two-dimensional view of power involves a *qualified critique* of the *behavioural focus* of the first view (I say qualified because it is still assumed that nondecision-making is a form of decision-making) and it allows for consideration of the ways in which *decisions* are prevented from being taken on *potential issues* over which there is an observable *conflict* of (subjective) *interests*, seen as embodied in express policy preferences and sub-political grievances.

20

4. THE THREE-DIMENSIONAL VIEW

THERE is no doubt that the two-dimensional view of power represents a major advance over the one-dimensional view : it incorporates into the analysis of power relations the question of the control over the agenda of politics and of the ways in which potential issues are kept out of the political process. None the less, it is, in my view, inadequate on three counts.

In the first place, its critique of behaviourism is too qualified, or, to put it another way, it is still too committed to behaviourism – that is, to the study of overt, 'actual behaviour', of which 'concrete decisions' in situations of conflict are seen as paradigmatic. In trying to assimilate all cases of exclusion of potential issues from the political agenda to the paradigm of a decision, it gives a misleading picture of the ways in which individuals and, above all, groups and institutions succeed in excluding potential issues from the political process. Decisions are choices consciously and intentionally made by individuals between alternatives, whereas the bias of the system can be mobilised, recreated and reinforced in ways that are neither consciously chosen nor the intended result of particular individuals' choices. As Bachrach and Baratz themselves maintain, the domination of defenders of the status quo may be so secure and pervasive that they are unaware of any potential challengers to their position and thus of any alternatives to the existing political process, whose bias they work to maintain. As 'students of power and its consequences', they write, 'our main concern is not whether the defenders of the status quo use their power consciously, but rather if and how they exercise it and what effects it has on the political process and other actors within the system' ([4] p. 50).

Moreover, the bias of the system is not sustained simply by a series of individually chosen acts, but also, most importantly, by the socially structured and culturally patterned behaviour of groups, and practices of institutions, which may indeed be manifested by individuals' inaction. Bachrach and Baratz follow the pluralists in adopting too methodologically individualist a view of power. In this both parties follow in the steps of Max Weber, for whom power was the probability of *individuals realising their wills* despite the resistance of others, whereas the power to control the agenda of politics and exclude potential issues cannot be adequately analysed unless it is seen as a function of collective forces and social arrangements.[1] There are, in fact, two separable cases here. First, there is the phenomenon of collective action, where the policy or action of a collectivity (whether a group, e.g. a class, or an institution, e.g. a political party or an industrial corporation) is manifest, but not attributable to particular individuals' decisions or behaviour. Second, there is the phenomenon of 'systemic' or organisational effects, where the mobilisation of bias results, as Schattschneider put it, from the form of organisation. Of course, such collectivities and organisations are made up of individuals – but the power they exercise cannot be simply conceptualised in terms of individuals' decisions or behaviour. As Marx succinctly put it, 'Men make their own history but they do not make it just as they please; they do not make it under circumstances chosen by themselves, but under circumstances directly encountered, given and transmitted from the past.'[2]

The second count on which the two-dimensional view of power is inadequate is in its association of power with actual, observable conflict. In this respect also the pluralists' critics follow their adversaries too closely[3] (and both in turn again follow Weber, who,

[1] See the present author's *Individualism* (Oxford: Blackwell, 1973) ch. 17. Contrast Dahrendorf's decision to 'follow . . . the useful and well-considered definitions of Max Weber', according to which 'the important difference between power and authority consists in the fact that whereas power is essentially tied to the personality of individuals, authority is always associated with social positions or roles' ([13] p. 166).
[2] Karl Marx and Friedrich Engels, 'The Eighteenth Brumaire of Louis Bonaparte', in Marx and Engels, *Selected Works* (Moscow: Foreign Languages Publishing House, 1962) vol. 1, p. 247.
[3] This association is made most clearly in *Power and Poverty* ([4] esp. pp. 49–50) in reaction to the pressure of pluralist criticisms of the (potentially three-dimensional) implications of the article on nondecisions [3]. See Merelman [20] and the Communications to the Editor of the *American Political Science Review*, 62 (1968) by Bachrach and Baratz (pp. 1268–9) and Merelman (p. 1269).

as we have seen, stressed the realisation of one's will, *despite the resistance of others*). This insistence on actual conflict as essential to power will not do, for at least two reasons.

The first is that, on Bachrach and Baratz's own analysis, two of the types of power may not involve such conflict : namely, manipulation and authority – which they conceive as 'agreement based upon reason' ([4] p. 20), though elsewhere they speak of it as involving a 'possible conflict of values' (p. 37).

The second reason why the insistence on actual and observable conflict will not do is simply that it is highly unsatisfactory to suppose that power is only exercised in situations of such conflict. To put the matter sharply, *A* may exercise power over *B* by getting him to do what he does not want to do, but he also exercises power over him by influencing, shaping or determining his very wants. Indeed, is it not the supreme exercise of power to get another or others to have the desires you want them to have – that is, to secure their compliance by controlling their thoughts and desires? One does not have to go to the lengths of talking about *Brave New World*, or the world of B. F. Skinner, to see this : thought control takes many less total and more mundane forms, through the control of information, through the mass media and through the processes of socialisation. Indeed, ironically, there are some excellent descriptions of this phenomenon in *Who Governs?* Consider the picture of the rule of the 'patricians' in the early nineteenth century : 'The elite seems to have possessed that most indispensable of all characteristics in a dominant group – the sense, shared not only by themselves but by the populace, that their claim to govern was legitimate' ([12] p. 17). And Dahl also sees this phenomenon at work under modern 'pluralist' conditions : leaders, he says, 'do not merely *respond* to the preferences of constituents; leaders also *shape* preferences' (p. 164), and, again, 'almost the entire adult population has been subjected to *some* degree of indoctrination through the schools' (p. 317), etc. The trouble seems to be that both Bachrach and Baratz and the pluralists suppose that because power, as they conceptualise it, only shows up in cases of actual conflict, it follows that actual conflict is necessary to power. But this is to ignore the crucial point that the most effective and insidious use of power is to prevent such conflict from arising in the first place.

The third count on which the two-dimensional view of power is inadequate is closely linked to the second : namely, its insistence that nondecision-making power only exists where there are grievances which are denied entry into the political process in the form of issues. If the observer can uncover no grievances, then he must assume there is a 'genuine' consensus on the prevailing allocation of values. To put this another way, it is here assumed that if men feel no grievances, then they have no interests that are harmed by the use of power. But this is also highly unsatisfactory. In the first place, what, in any case, is a grievance – an articulated demand, based on political knowledge, an undirected complaint arising out of everyday experience, a vague feeling of unease or sense of deprivation? (See [18].) Second, and more important, is it not the supreme and most insidious exercise of power to prevent people, to whatever degree, from having grievances by shaping their perceptions, cognitions and preferences in such a way that they accept their role in the existing order of things, either because they can see or imagine no alternative to it, or because they see it as natural and unchangeable, or because they value it as divinely ordained and beneficial? To assume that the absence of grievance equals genuine consensus is simply to rule out the possibility of false or manipulated consensus by definitional fiat.

☞ In summary, the three-dimensional view of power involves a *thoroughgoing critique* of the *behavioural focus*[4] of the first two views as too individualistic and allows for consideration of the many ways in which *potential issues* are kept out of politics, whether through the operation of social forces and institutional practices or through individuals' decisions. This, moreover, can occur in the absence of actual, observable conflict, which may have been successfully averted – though there remains here an implicit reference to potential conflict. This potential, however, may never in fact be actualised. What one may have here is a *latent conflict*, which consists in a contradiction between the in-

---

[4] I use the term 'behavioural' in the narrow sense indicated above, to refer to the study of overt and actual behaviour – and specifically concrete decisions. Of course, in the widest sense, the three-dimensional view of power is 'behavioural' in that it is committed to the view that behaviour (action and inaction, conscious and unconscious, actual and potential) provides evidence (direct and indirect) for an attribution of the exercise of power.

terests of those exercising power and the *real interests* of those they exclude.[5] These latter may not express or even be conscious of their interests, but, as I shall argue, the identification of those interests ultimately always rests on empirically supportable and refutable hypotheses.

The distinctive features of the three views of power presented above are summarised below.

One-Dimensional View of Power

Focus on (a) behaviour
         (b) decision-making
         (c) (key) issues
         (d) observable (overt) conflict
         (e) (subjective) interests, seen as policy preferences revealed by political participation

Two-Dimensional View of Power

(Qualified) critique of behavioural focus
Focus on (a) decision-making and nondecision-making
         (b) issues and potential issues
         (c) observable (overt or covert) conflict
         (d) (subjective) interests, seen as policy preferences or grievances

Three-Dimensional View of Power

Critique of behavioural focus
Focus on (a) decision-making and control over political agenda (not necessarily through decisions)
         (b) issues and potential issues
         (c) observable (overt or covert) and latent conflict
         (d) subjective and real interests

---

[5] This conflict is latent in the sense that it is assumed that there *would be* a conflict of wants or preferences between those exercising power and those subject to it, were the latter to become aware of their interests. (My account of latent conflict and real interests is to be distinguished from Dahrendorf's account of 'objective' and 'latent' interests as 'antagonistic interests conditioned by, even inherent in, social positions', in imperatively co-ordinated associations, which are 'independent of [the individual's] conscious orientations' ([13] pp. 174, 178). Dahrendorf assumes as sociologically given what I claim to be empirically ascertainable.)

5. THE UNDERLYING CONCEPT OF POWER

ONE feature which these three views of power share is their evaluative character : each arises out of and operates within a particular moral and political perspective. Indeed, I would maintain that power is one of those concepts which is ineradicably value-dependent. By this I mean that both its very definition and any given use of it, once defined, are inextricably tied to a given set of (probably unacknowledged) value-assumptions which predetermine the range of its empirical application – and I shall maintain below that some such uses permit that range to extend further and deeper than others. Moreover, the concept of power is, in consequence, what has been called an 'essentially contested concept' – one of those concepts which 'inevitably involve endless disputes about their proper uses on the part of their users' ([15] p. 169). Indeed, to engage in such disputes is itself to engage in politics.

The absolutely basic common core to, or primitive notion lying behind, all talk of power is the notion that A in some way affects B. But, in applying that primitive (causal) notion to the analysis of social life, something further is needed – namely, the notion that A does so in a non-trivial or significant manner (see [36]). Clearly, we all affect each other in countless ways all the time : the concept of power, and the related concepts of coercion, influence, authority, etc., pick out ranges of such affecting as being significant in specific ways. A way of conceiving power (or a way of defining the concept of power) that will be useful in the analysis of social relationships must imply an answer to the question : 'what counts as a significant manner?', 'what makes A's affecting B significant?' Now, the *concept* of power, thus defined, when interpreted and put to work, yields one or more *views* of power – that is, ways of identifying cases of power in the real world. The three views we have been considering can be seen as alternative interpretations and applications of one and the same underlying concept of power, according to which *A* exercises power over *B* when *A* affects *B* in a manner contrary to *B*'s interests.[1] There are, however, alternative (no less contestable) ways of conceptualising power, involving alternative criteria of significance. Let us look at two of them.

Consider, first, the concept of power elaborated by Talcott Parsons [26, 27, 28, 29]. Parsons seeks to 'treat power as a *specific* mechanism operating to bring about changes in the action of other units, individual or collective, in the processes of social interaction' ([28], in [29] p. 299). What is it, in his view, that is specific about this mechanism, which distinguishes it as 'power'? In other words, what criteria of significance does Parsons use to identify a particular range of affecting as 'power'? The answer is, in a nutshell, the use of authoritative decisions to further collective goals. He defines power thus :

Power then is generalized capacity to secure the performance

---

[1] This distinction between 'concept' and 'view' is closely parallel to that drawn by John Rawls between 'concept' and 'conception'. It seems, writes Rawls,

natural to think of the concept of justice as distinct from the various conceptions of justice and as being specified by the role which these different sets of principles, these different conceptions, have in common. Those who hold different conceptions of justice can, then, still agree that institutions are just when no arbitrary distinctions are made between persons in the assigning of basic rights and duties and when the rules determine a proper balance between competing claims to the advantages of social life. Men can agree to this description of just institutions since the notions of an arbitrary distinction and of a proper balance, which are included in the concept of justice, are left open for each to interpret according to the principles of justice that he accepts. These principles single out which similarities and differences among persons are relevant in determining rights and duties and they specify which division of advantages is appropriate. (John Rawls, *A Theory of Justice*, Oxford: Clarendon Press, 1972, pp. 5–6.)

Analogously, those holding the three different views of power I have set out offer differing interpretations of what are to count as interests and how they may be adversely affected. I further agree with Rawls's suggestions that the various conceptions of justice (like views of power) are 'the outgrowth of different notions of society against the background of opposing views of the natural necessities and opportunities of human life. Fully to understand a conception of justice we must make explicit the conception of social co-operation from which it derives' (pp. 9–10). I disagree, however, with Rawls's apparent belief that there is ultimately one rational conception or set of principles of justice to be discovered. 'Justice' is no less essentially contested than 'power'.

of binding obligations by units in a system of collective organization when the obligations are legitimized with reference to their bearing on collective goals and where in case of recalcitrance there is a presumption of enforcement by negative situational sanctions – whatever the actual agency of that enforcement (p. 308).

The 'power of A over B is, in its legitimized form, the "right" of A, as a decision-making unit involved in collective process, to make decisions which take precedence over those of B, in the interest of the effectiveness of the collective operation as a whole' (p. 318).

Parsons's conceptualisation of power ties it to authority, consensus and the pursuit of collective goals, and dissociates it from conflicts of interest and, in particular, from coercion and force. Thus power depends on 'the institutionalization of authority' (p. 331) and is 'conceived as a generalized medium of mobilizing commitments or obligation for effective collective action' (p. 331). By contrast, 'the threat of coercive measures, or of compulsion, without legitimation or justification, should not properly be called the use of power at all. . . .' (p. 331). Thus Parsons criticised Wright Mills for interpreting power 'exclusively as a facility for getting what one group, the holders of power, wants by preventing another group, the "outs" from getting what it wants', rather than seeing it as 'a facility for the performance of function in and on behalf of the society as a system' ([26] p. 139).

Consider, secondly, the concept of power as def ed by Hannah Arendt. '*Power*', she writes,

corresponds to the human ability not just to act but to act in concert. Power is never the property of an individual; it belongs to a group and remains in existence only so long as the group keeps together. When we say of somebody that he is 'in power' we actually refer to his being empowered by a certain number of people to act in their name. The moment the group, from which the power originated to begin with (*potestas in populo*, without a people or group there is no power), disappears, 'his power' also vanishes. ([1] p. 44)

It is

> the people's support that lends power to the institutions of a
> country, and this support is but the continuation of the con-
> sent that brought the laws into existence to begin with. Under
> conditions of representative government the people are sup-
> posed to rule those who govern them. All political institutions
> are manifestations and materializations of power; they petrify
> and decay as soon as the living power of the people ceases to
> uphold them. This is what Madison meant when he said 'all
> governments rest on opinion', a word no less true for the vari-
> ous forms of monarchy than for democracies. (p. 41)

Arendt's way of conceiving power ties it to a tradition and a
vocabulary which she traces back to Athens and Rome, according to which the republic is based on the rule of law, which rests
on 'the power of the people' (p. 40). In this perspective power
is dissociated from 'the command–obedience relationship' (p.40)
and 'the business of dominion' (p. 44). Power is consensual :
it 'needs no justification, being inherent in the very existence of
political communities; what it does need is legitimacy. . . . Power
springs up whenever people get together and act in concert, but
it derives its legitimacy from the initial getting together rather
than from any action that then may follow' (p. 52). *Violence*,
by contrast, is instrumental, a means to an end, but 'never will
be legitimate' (p. 52). Power, 'far from being the means to an
end, is actually the very condition enabling a group of people
to think and act in terms of the means–end category' (p. 51).

The *point* of these rather similar definitions of power by Parsons and Arendt is to lend persuasive support to the general theoretical frameworks of their authors. In Parsons's case the linking
of power to authoritative decisions and collective goals serves
to reinforce his theory of social integration as based on value consensus by concealing from view the whole range of problems that
have concerned so-called 'coercion' theorists, precisely under the
rubric of 'power'. By definitional fiat, phenomena of coercion,
exploitation, manipulation and so on cease to be phenomena
of power – and in consequence disappear from the theoretical landscape. Anthony Giddens has put this point very well :

29

Two obvious facts, that authoritative decisions very often do serve sectional interests and that the most radical conflicts in society stem from struggles for power, are defined out of consideration – at least as phenomena connected with 'power'. The conceptualisation of power which Parsons offers allows him to shift the entire weight of his analysis away from power as expressing a relation *between* individuals or groups, toward seeing power as a 'system property'. That collective 'goals', or even the values which lie behind them, may be the outcome of a 'negotiated order' built on conflicts between parties holding differential power is ignored, since for Parsons 'power' assumes the prior existence of collective goals. ([16] p. 265)

In the case of Arendt, similarly, the conceptualisation of power plays a persuasive role, in defence of her conception of 'the *res publica*, the public thing' to which people consent and 'behave nonviolently and argue rationally', and in opposition to the reduction of 'public affairs to the business of dominion' and to the conceptual linkage of power with force and violence. To 'speak of non-violent power', she writes, 'is actually redundant' ([1] p. 56). These distinctions enable Arendt to make statements such as the following: 'tyranny, as Montesquieu discovered, is therefore the most violent and least powerful of forms of government' (p. 41); 'Where power has disintegrated, revolutions are possible but not necessary' (p. 49); 'Even the most despotic domination we know of, the rule of master over slaves, who always outnumbered him, did not rest on superior means of coercion as such, but on a superior organization of power – that is, on the organized solidarity of the masters' (p. 50); 'Violence can always destroy power; out of the barrel of a gun grows the most effective command, resulting in the most instant and perfect obedience. What can never grow out of it is power' (p. 53); 'Power and violence are opposites; where the one rules absolutely, the other is absent. Violence appears where power is in jeopardy, but left to its own course it ends in power's disappearance' (p. 56).

These conceptualisations of power are rationally defensible. It is, however, the contention of this book that they are of less value than that advanced here for two reasons.

In the first place, they are revisionary persuasive redefinitions of power which are out of line with the central meanings of 'power' as traditionally understood and with the concerns that have always centrally preoccupied students of power. They focus on the locution 'power to', ignoring 'power over'. Thus power indicates a 'capacity', a 'facility', an 'ability', not a relationship. Accordingly, the conflictual aspect of power – the fact that it is exercised *over* people – disappears altogether from view.[2] And along with it there disappears the central interest of studying power relations in the first place – an interest in the (attempted or successful) securing of people's compliance by overcoming or averting their opposition.

In the second place, the point of these definitions is, as we have seen, to reinforce certain theoretical positions; but everything that can be said by their means can be said with greater clarity by means of the conceptual scheme here proposed, without thereby concealing from view the (central) aspects of power which they define out of existence. Thus, for instance, Parsons objects to seeing power as a 'zero-sum' phenomenon and appeals to the analogy of credit creation in the economy, arguing that the use of power, as when the ruled have justified confidence in their rulers, may achieve objectives which all desire and from which all benefit. It has been argued in defence of this view that 'in any type of group, the existence of defined "leadership" positions does "generate" power which may be used to achieve aims desired by the majority of the members of the group' ([16] p. 263). Similarly, Arendt wants to say that members of a group acting in concert are exercising power. According to the conceptual scheme here advanced, all such cases of co-operative activity, where individuals or groups significantly affect one another in the absence of a conflict of interests between them, will be identifiable, as cases of 'influence' but not of 'power'. All that Parsons and Arendt wish to say about consensual behaviour remains sayable, but so also does all that they wish to remove from the language of power.

It may be useful if at this point I set out a conceptual map (Fig. 1) of power and its cognates (all modes of 'significant affecting') – a map which broadly follows Bachrach and

---

[2] Thus for Parsons 'the power of A over B' becomes a 'right' of precedence in decision-making!

Baratz's typology, referred to above. Needless to say, this map is itself essentially contestable – and, in particular, although it is meant to analyse and situate the concept of power which under-lies the one-, two- and three-dimensional views of power, I do not claim that it would necessarily be acceptable to all the pro-ponents of those respective views. One reason for that, of course, is that it is developed from the perspective of the three-dimen-sional view, which incorporates and therefore goes further than the other two.

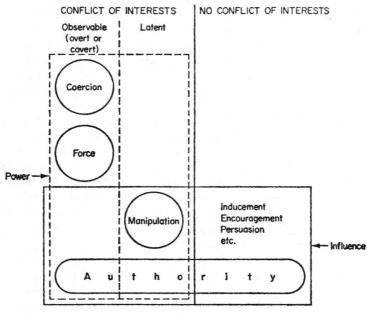

Fig. 1

It will be seen that in this scheme power may or may not be a form of influence – depending on whether sanctions are involved; while influence and authority may or may not be a form of power – depending on whether a conflict of interests is involved. Consensual authority, with no conflict of interests, is not, there-fore, a form of power.

The question of whether rational persuasion is a form of power

32

and influence cannot be adequately treated here. For what it is worth, my inclination is to say both yes and no. Yes, because it is a form of significant affecting: *A* gets (causes) *B* to do or think what he would not otherwise do or think. No, because *B* autonomously accepts *A*'s reasons, so that one is inclined to say that it is not *A* but *A*'s reasons, or *B*'s acceptance of them, that is responsible for *B*'s change of course. I suspect that we are here in the presence of a fundamental (Kantian) antinomy between causality, on the one hand, and autonomy and reason, on the other. I see no way of resolving this antinomy: there are simply contradictory conceptual pressures at work.

It may further be asked whether power can be exercised by *A* over *B* in *B*'s real interests. That is, suppose there is a conflict now between the preferences of *A* and *B*, but that *A*'s preferences are in *B*'s real interests. To this there are two possible responses: (1) that *A* might exercise 'short-term power' over *B* (with an observable conflict of subjective interests), but that if and when *B* recognises his real interests, the power relation ends: it is self-annihilating; or (2) that all or most forms of attempted or successful control by *A* over *B*, when *B* objects or resists, constitute a violation of *B*'s autonomy; that *B* has a real interest in his own autonomy; so that such an exercise of power cannot be in *B*'s real interests. Clearly the first of these responses is open to misuse by seeming to provide a paternalist licence for tyranny; while the second furnishes an anarchist defence against it, collapsing all or most cases of influence into power. Though attracted by the second, I am inclined to adopt the first, the dangers of which may be obviated by insisting on the empirical basis for identifying real interests. The identification of these is not up to *A*, *but to B*, exercising choice under conditions of relative autonomy and, in particular, independently of *A*'s power – e.g. through democratic participation.[3]

---

[2] On this last point, see the past and future writings of Peter Bachrach.

33

6. POWER AND INTERESTS

I HAVE defined the concept of power by saying that A exercises power over B when A affects B in a manner contrary to B's interests. Now the notion of 'interests' is an irreducibly evaluative notion (see [8] and [5]): if I say that something is in your interests, I imply that you have a prima facie claim to it, and if I say that 'policy x is in A's interest' this constitutes a prima facie justification for that policy. In general, talk of interests provides a licence for the making of normative judgments of a moral and political character. So it is not surprising that different conceptions of what interests *are* are associated with different moral and political positions. Extremely crudely, one might say that the liberal takes men as they are and applies want-regarding principles to them, relating their interests to what they actually want or prefer, to their policy preferences as manifested by their political participation.[1] The reformist, seeing and deploring that not all men's wants are given equal weight by the political system, also relates their interests to what they want or prefer, but allows that this may be revealed in more indirect and sub-political ways – in the form of deflected, submerged or concealed wants and preferences. The radical, however, maintains that men's wants may themselves be a product of a system which works against their interests, and, in such cases, relates the latter to what they would want and prefer, were they able to make the choice.[2] Each

[1] See Brian Barry, *Political Argument* (London: Routledge & Kegan Paul, 1965) and the present author's discussion of it in 'Varieties of Political Philosophy', *Political Studies*, 15 (1967) pp. 55–9.

[2] Cf. Connolly's 'first approximation' to a definition of real interests: 'Policy x is more in A's interest than policy y, if A were he to experience the *results* of both x and y, would *choose* x as the result he would rather have for himself' ([8] p. 472). I too connect real interests with (relative) autonomy and choice. What is, of

of these three picks out a certain range of the entire class of actual and potential wants as the relevant object of his moral appraisal. In brief, my suggestion is that the one-dimensional view of power presupposes a liberal conception of interests, the two-dimensional view a reformist conception, and the three-dimensional view a radical conception. (And I would maintain that any view of power rests on some normatively specific conception of interests.)[3]

course, required at this point is a sustained discussion of the nature of, and conditions for, autonomy (and its relation to social determination). The reader will find the beginnings of such a discussion in the author's *Individualism*, chs. 8, 18 and 20.

[3] See the present author's paper 'Relativism: Cognitive and Moral', *Supplementary Proceedings of the Aristotelian Society* (June 1974).

7. THE THREE VIEWS COMPARED

I NOW turn to consider the relative strengths and weaknesses of the three views of power I have outlined.

The virtues of the decision-making or one-dimensional view are obvious and have often been stressed : by means of it, to cite Merelman again, the pluralists 'studied actual behavior, stressed operational definitions, and turned up evidence' ([20] p. 451). However, the trouble is that, by doing this, by studying the making of important decisions within the community, they were simply taking over and reproducing the bias of the system they were studying. By analysing the decisions on urban redevelopment, public education and political nominations, Dahl tells us a good deal about the *diversity* of decision-making power in New Haven. He shows that these issue areas are independent of one another, and that, by and large, different individuals exercise power in different areas and therefore no set of individuals and thus no single elite has decision-making power ranging across different issue areas. He further argues that the decision-making process is responsive to the preferences of citizens because the elected politicians and officials engaged in it anticipate the results of future elections. It would, he writes, 'be unwise to underestimate the extent to which voters may exert *indirect* influence on the decisions of leaders by means of elections ([12] p. 101): no issue of importance to the former is likely to be ignored for long by the latter. Thus Dahl pictures pluralist politics as both diverse and open : he writes, '[T]he independence, penetrability, and heterogeneity of the various segments of the political stratum all but guarantee that any dissatisfied group will find spokesmen in the political stratum' (p. 93). But the diversity and openness

Dahl sees may be highly misleading if power is being exercised within the system to limit decision-making to acceptable issues. Individuals and elites may act separately in making acceptable decisions, but they may act in concert – or even fail to act at all – in such a way as to keep unacceptable issues out of politics, thereby preventing the system from becoming any more diverse than it is. 'A polity', it has been suggested, 'that is pluralistic in its decision-making can be unified in its non-decisionmaking' ([9] p. 179). The decision-making method prevents this possibility from being considered. Dahl concludes that the system is penetrable by any dissatisfied group, but he does so only by studying cases of successful penetration, and never examines failed attempts at such penetration. Moreover, the thesis that indirect influence gives the electorate control over leaders can be turned on its head. Indirect influence can equally operate to prevent politicians, officials or others from raising issues or proposals known to be unacceptable to some group or institution in the community. It can serve the interests of an elite, not only that of the electorate. In brief, the one-dimensional view of power cannot reveal the less visible ways in which a pluralist system may be biased in favour of certain groups and against others.

The two-dimensional view goes some way to revealing this – which is a considerable advance in itself – but it confines itself to studying situations where the mobilisation of bias can be attributed to individuals' decisions that have the effect of preventing currently observable grievances (overt or covert) from becoming issues within the political process. This, I think, largely accounts for the very thin and inadequate character of Bachrach and Baratz's study of poverty, race and politics in Baltimore. All that study really amounts to is an account of various decisions by the mayor and various business leaders to deflect the inchoate demands of Baltimore's blacks from becoming politically threatening issues – by such devices as making certain appointments, establishing task forces to defuse the poverty issue, by supporting certain kinds of welfare measures, etc. – together with an account of how the blacks gained political access through overt struggle involving riots. The analysis remains superficial precisely because it confines itself to studying individual decisions made to avert potentially threatening demands from becoming politically dangerous. A deeper analysis would also concern itself with all the complex and subtle ways in which the *inactivity* of leaders and the sheer weight of institutions – political, industrial and educational – served for so long to keep the blacks out of Baltimore politics; and indeed for a long period kept them from even trying to get into it.

The three-dimensional view offers the possibility of such an analysis. It offers, in other words, the prospect of a serious sociological and not merely personalised explanation of how political systems prevent demands from becoming political issues or even from being made. Now the classical objection to doing this has often been stated by pluralists: how can one study, let alone explain, what does not happen? Polsby writes:

> . . . it has been suggested that non-events make more significant policy than do policy-making events. This is the kind of statement that has a certain plausibility and attractiveness but that presents truly insuperable obstacles to research. We can sound the depth of the abyss very quickly by agreeing that non-events are much more important than events, and inquiring precisely *which* non-events are to be regarded as most significant in the community. Surely not *all* of them. For every event (no matter how defined) that occurs there must be an infinity of alternatives. Then which non-events are to be regarded as significant? One satisfactory answer might be: those outcomes desired by a significant number of actors in the community but not achieved. Insofar as these goals are in some way explicitly pursued by people in the community, the method of study used in New Haven has a reasonable chance of capturing them. A wholly unsatisfactory answer would be: certain non-events stipulated by outside observers without reference to the desires or activities of community residents. The answer is unsatisfactory because it is obviously inappropriate for outsiders to pick among all the possible outcomes that did not take place a set which they regard as important but which community citizens do not. This approach is likely to prejudice the outcomes of research. . . . ([30] pp. 96–7)

Similarly, Wolfinger argues that the 'infinite variety of possible nondecisions . . . reveals the idea's adaptability to various ideological perspectives' ([37] p. 1078). Moreover, suppose we advance 'a theory of political interests and rational behavior' specifying how people would behave in certain situations if left to themselves, and use it to support the claim that their failure so to behave is due to the exercise of power. In this case, Wolfinger argues, we have no means of deciding between two possibilities: either that there was an exercise of power, or that the theory was wrong (p. 1078).

The first point to be made against these apparently powerful arguments is that they move from a methodological difficulty to a substantive assertion. It does not follow that, just because it is difficult or even impossible to show that power has been exercised in a given situation, we can conclude that it has not. But, more importantly, I do not believe that it is impossible to identify an exercise of power of this type.

What is an exercise of power? What is it to exercise power? On close inspection it turns out that the locution 'exercise of power' and 'exercising power' is problematic in at least two ways.

In the first place, it carries, in everyday usage, a doubly unfortunate connotation: it is sometimes assumed to be both individualistic and intentional, that is, it seems to carry the suggestion that the exercise of power is a matter of individuals consciously acting to affect others. Some appear to feel discomfort in speaking either of groups, institutions, or collectivities 'exercising' power, or of individuals or collectivities doing so unconsciously. This is an interesting case of individualistic and intentional assumptions being built into our language – but that in itself provides no reason for adopting such assumptions. In what follows I propose to abandon these assumptions and to speak of the exercise of power whether by individuals or by groups, institutions, etc., and whether consciously or not. A negative justification for this revisionary usage is that there is no other available word that meets the bill (thus 'exerting' power is little different from 'exercising' it); I shall offer a positive justification below.

The second way in which the phrase 'exercising-power' is problematic is that it conceals an interesting and important ambiguity. I referred above to Dahl's definition of the exercise of power in terms of A getting B to do something he would not otherwise do. However, this is, as it stands, too simple.

Suppose that A can *normally* affect B. This is to suppose that, against the background of (what is assumed to be) a normally ongoing situation, if A does x, he gets B to do what he would not otherwise· do. Here A's action, x, is *sufficient* to get B to do what he would not otherwise do. Suppose, however, that exactly the same is true of A_1. He can also normally affect B: his action, y, is also sufficient to get B to do what he would not otherwise do, in just the same way. Now, suppose that A and A_1 both act in relation to B simultaneously and B changes his action accordingly. Here, it is clear, B's action or change of course is overdetermined: both A and A_1 have affected B by 'exercising power', but the result is the same as that which would have occurred had either affected him singly. In this case it is a pointless question to ask which of them produced the change of course, that is, which of them made a difference to the result: they both did. They both 'exercised power', in a sense – that is, a power *sufficient* to produce the result, yet one cannot say that *either* of them made a difference to the result. Let us call this sense of 'exercising power' the *operative* sense.

Contrast this case with the case where A *does* make a difference to the result: that is, against the background of a normally ongoing situation, A, by doing x, actually gets B to do what B would not otherwise do. Here x is an intervening cause which distorts the normal course of events – by contrast with the first, overdetermined case, where there are, *ex hypothesi, two* intervening sufficient conditions, so that neither can be said to have 'made a difference', just because of the presence of the other: there the normal course of events is itself distorted by the presence of the other intervening sufficient condition. In this case, by contrast, A's intervention can be said to make a difference to the result. Let us call this sense of 'exercising power' the *effective* sense.

(It is worth adding a further distinction, which turns on *what* difference A makes to the result. A wishes B to do some particular thing, but, in exercising effective power over him, he may succeed in changing B's course in a wide variety of ways. Only in the case where B's change of course corresponds to A's wishes, that is, where A secures B's compliance, can we speak properly of a *successful* exercise of power: here 'affecting' becomes 'control'. It is, incidentally, this case of the successful exercise of power, or the securing of compliance, on which Bachrach and Baratz exclusively concentrate. The successful exercise of power can be seen as a sub-species of the effective exercise of power – though one could maintain that, where the operative exercise of power issues in compliance, this also is an [indeterminate] form of its successful exercise.)

We can now turn to the analysis of what exactly is involved in identifying an exercise of power. An attribution of the exercise of power involves, among other things, the double claim that A acts (or fails to act) in a certain way and that B does what he would not otherwise do (I use the term 'do' here in a very wide sense, to include 'think', 'want', 'feel', etc.). In the case of an effective exercise of power, A gets B to do what he would not otherwise do; in the case of an operative exercise of power, A, together with another or other sufficient conditions, gets B to do what he would not otherwise do. Hence, in general, any attribution of the exercise of power (including, of course, those by Dahl and his colleagues) always implies a relevant counterfactual, to the effect that (but for A, or but for A together with any other sufficient conditions) B would otherwise have done, let us say, b. This is one reason why so many thinkers (mistakenly) insist on actual, observable conflict as essential to power (though there are doubtless other theoretical and, indeed, ideological reasons). For such conflict provides the relevant counterfactual, so to speak, ready-made. If A and B are in conflict with one another, A wanting a and B wanting b, then if A prevails over B, we can assume that B would otherwise have done b. Where there is no observable conflict between A and B, then we must provide other grounds for asserting the relevant counterfactual. That is, we must provide other, indirect, grounds for asserting that if A had not acted (or failed to act) in a certain way – and, in the case of operative power, if other sufficient conditions had not been operative – then B would have thought and acted differently from the way he does actually think and act. In brief, we need to justify our expectation that B would have thought or acted differently; and we also need to specify the means or mechanism by which A has prevented, or else acted (or abstained from acting) in a manner sufficient to prevent, B from doing so.

I can see no reason to suppose that either of these claims cannot in principle be supported – though I do not claim it is easy. Doing so certainly requires one to go much deeper than most analyses of power in contemporary political science and sociology. Fortunately, Matthew Crenson's book, *The Un-Politics of Air Pollution: A Study of Non-Decisionmaking in the Cities* [9], provides a good example of how the task can be approached. The theoretical framework of this book can be seen as lying on the borderline of the two-dimensional and the three-dimensional views of power : I see it as a serious attempt empirically to apply the former, together with certain elements of the latter. For that reason, it marks a real theoretical advance in the empirical study of power relations.

It explicitly attempts to find a way to explain 'things that do not happen', on the assumption that 'the proper object of investigation is not political activity but political inactivity' (pp. vii, 26). Why, he asks, was the issue of air pollution not raised as early or as effectively in some American cities as it was in others? His object, in other words, is to 'discover . . . why many cities and towns in the United States failed to make a political issue of their air pollution problems' (p. vii), thereby illuminating the character of local political systems – particularly with respect to their 'penetrability'. He first shows that differences in the treatment of pollution cannot be attributed solely to differences in the actual pollution level or to social characteristics of the populations in question. He then provides a detailed study of two neighbouring cities in Indiana, both equally polluted and with similar populations, one of which, East Chicago, took action to clear its air in 1949, while the other, Gary, held its breath until 1962. Briefly, his explanation of the difference is that Gary is a one-company town dominated by U.S. Steel, with a strong party organisation, whereas East Chicago had a number of steel companies and no strong party organisation when it passed its air pollution control ordinance.

His case (which he documents with convincing detail) is that U.S. Steel, which had built Gary and was responsible for its prosperity, for a long time effectively prevented the issue from even

being raised, through its power reputation operating on antici-
pated reactions, then for a number of years thwarted attempts
to raise the issue, and decisively influenced the content of the
anti-pollution ordinance finally enacted. Moreover, it did all this
without acting or entering into the political arena. Its 'mere reputation for power, unsupported by acts of power' was 'sufficient
to inhibit the emergence of the dirty air issue' (p. 124); and,
when it eventually did emerge (largely because of the threat of
Federal or State action), 'U.S. Steel . . . influenced the content of
the pollution ordinance without taking any action on it, and thus
defied the pluralist dictum that political power belongs to political actors' (pp. 69–70). U.S. Steel, Crenson argues, exercised
influence 'from points outside the range of observable political
behaviour. . . . Though the corporation seldom intervened directly
in the deliberations of the town's air pollution policymakers, it
was nevertheless able to affect their scope and direction' (p. 107).
He writes :

Gary's anti-pollution activists were long unable to get U.S.
Steel to take a clear stand. One of them, looking back on the
bleak days of the dirty air debate, cited the evasiveness of the
town's largest industrial corporation as a decisive factor in
frustrating early efforts to enact a pollution control ordinance.
The company executives, he said, would just nod sympathetic-
ally 'and agree that air pollution was terrible, and pat you on
the head. But they never *did* anything one way or the other.
If only there had been a fight, then something might have
been accomplished!' What U.S. Steel did not do was probably
more important to the career of Gary's air pollution issue than
what it did do. (pp. 76–7)

He then moves from these two detailed case studies to a comparative analysis of interview data with political leaders taken
from fifty-one cities, aimed at testing the hypotheses arising out
of the two case studies. Briefly, his conclusions are that 'the air
pollution issue tends not to flourish in cities where industry en-
joys a reputation for power' (p. 145) – and that 'where industry
remains silent about dirty air, the life chances of the pollution
issue are likely to be diminished' (p. 124). Again, a strong and

43

influential party organisation will also inhibit the growth of the pollution issue, since demands for clean air are unlikely to yield the kind of specific benefits that American party machines seek – though where industry has a high power reputation, a strong party will increase the pollution issue's life chances, since it will seek to purchase industrial influence. In general Crenson plausibly argues that pollution control is a good example of a collective good, whose specific costs are concentrated on industry : thus the latter's opposition will be strong, while the support for it will be relatively weak, since its benefits are diffuse and likely to have little appeal to party leaders engaged in influence brokerage. Moreover, and very interestingly, Crenson argues, against the pluralists, that political issues tend to be interconnected; and thus collective issues tend to promote other collective issues, and vice versa. Thus by 'promoting one political agenda item, civic activists may succeed in driving other issues away' (p. 170):

> where business and industrial development is a topic of local concern, the dirty air problem tends to be ignored. The prominence of one issue appears to be connected with the sub- ᵓrdination of the other, and the existence of this connection calls into question the pluralist view that different political issues tend to rise and subside independently. (p. 165)

Crenson's general case is that there are 'politically imposed limitations upon the scope of decision-making', such that 'decision-making activity is channelled and directed by the process of non-decision-making' (p. 178). Pluralism, in other words, is 'no guarantee of political openness or popular sovereignty'; and neither the study of decision-making nor the existence of 'visible diversity' will tell us anything about 'those groups and issues which may have been shut out of a town's political life' (p. 181).

I suggested above that the theoretical framework of Crenson's analysis lies on the borderline of the two-dimensional and the three-dimensional views of power. It is, on the face of it, a two-dimensional study of nondecision-making à la Bachrach and Baratz. On the other hand, it begins to advance beyond their position (as presented in their book) in three ways. First, it does not interpret nondecision-making behaviourally, as exhibited only in decisions (hence the stress on inaction – 'What U.S. Steel did not do . . .'); second, it is non-individualistic and considers institutional power;[1] and third, it considers ways in which demands are prevented, through the exercise of such power, from being raised : thus,

> Local political forms and practices may even inhibit citizens' ability to transform some diffuse discontent into an explicit demand. In short, there is something like an inarticulate ideology in political institutions, even in those that appear to be most open-minded, flexible and disjointed – an ideology in the sense that it promotes the selective perception and articulation of social problems and conflicts. . . . (p. 23)

In this way, 'local political institutions and political leaders may . . . exercise considerable control over what people choose to care about and how forcefully they articulate their cares' (p. 27): restrictions on the scope of decision-making may 'stunt the political consciousness of the local public' by confining minority opinions to minorities and denying 'minorities the opportunity to grow to majorities' (pp. 180–1).

Crenson's analysis is impressive because it fulfils the double requirement mentioned above : there is good reason to expect that, other things being equal, people would rather not be poisoned (assuming, in particular, that pollution control does not necessarily mean unemployment) – even where they may not even articulate this preference; and hard evidence is given of the ways in which institutions, specifically U.S. Steel, largely through inaction, prevented the citizens' interest in not being poisoned from being acted on (though other factors, institutional and ideological, would need to enter a fuller explanation). Thus both the relevant counterfactual and the identification of a power mechanism are justified.

---

[1] On the other hand, Crenson's use of the reputational method for locating power does lead him to focus on the *motives* of industrialists, political leaders, etc. and thus to ignore 'the possibility of more impersonal, structural and systematic explanations', such as that 'certain forms of city government in the United States are poorly adapted to handle this particular issue' of air pollution (K. Newton, review of Crenson, op. cit., *Political Studies*, 20 (1972) p. 487).

8. DIFFICULTIES

I WISH, however, to conclude on a problematic note, by alluding to the difficulties, peculiar to the three-dimensional view of power, first, of justifying the relevant counterfactual, and second, of identifying the mechanism or process of an alleged exercise of power.

In the first place, justifying the relevant counterfactual is not always as easy or as clearcut as in the case of air pollution in Gary, Indiana. There are a number of features of that case that may not be present in others. First, the value judgment implicit in the specification of Gary's citizens' interest in not being poisoned is scarcely disputable – resting, as Crenson says, on 'the opinion of the observer concerning the value of human life' (p. 3). Second, the empirical hypothesis that those citizens, if they had the choice and fuller information, would prefer not to be poisoned is more than plausible (on the assumption that such an alternative did not entail increased unemployment). And third, Crenson's study provides comparative data to support the claim that, under different conditions where the alleged nondecisional power was not operative, or operative to a lesser degree, people with comparable social characteristics did make and enforce that choice, or did so with less difficulty.[1]

Sometimes, however, it is extraordinarily difficult to justify the relevant counterfactual. Can we always assume that the victims of injustice and inequality would, but for the exercise of power, strive for justice and equality? What about the cultural relativity

[1] However, it should be noted that his statistical correlations are rather low (the highest being 0·61, and most being between 0·20 and 0·40). Strictly speaking, Crenson offers only highly plausible hypotheses which are not controverted by his evidence but only weakly supported by it.

of values? Is not such an assumption a form of ethnocentrism? Why not say that acquiescence in a value system 'we' reject, such as orthodox communism or the caste system, is a case of genuine consensus over different values? But even here empirical support is not beyond our reach. It is not impossible to adduce evidence – which must, by nature of the case, be indirect – to support the claim that an apparent case of consensus is not genuine but imposed (though there will be mixed cases, with respect to different groups and different components of the value system).

Where is such evidence to be found? There is a most interesting passage in Antonio Gramsci's *Prison Notebooks* which bears on this question, where Gramsci draws a contrast between 'thought and action, i.e. the co-existence of two conceptions of the world, one affirmed in words and the other displayed in effective action' ([17] p. 326). Where this contrast occurs 'in the life of great masses', Gramsci writes, it

> cannot but be the expression of profounder contrasts of a social historical order. It signifies that the social group in question may indeed have its own conception of the world, even if only embryonic; a conception which manifests itself in action, but occasionally and in flashes – when, that is, the group is acting as an organic totality. But this same group has, for reasons of submission and intellectual subordination, adopted a conception which is not its own but is borrowed from another group; and it affirms this conception verbally and believes itself to be following it, because this is the conception which it follows in 'normal times' – that is when its conduct is not independent and autonomous, but submissive and subordinate. (p. 327)[2]

Although one may not accept Gramsci's attribution of 'its own conception of the world' to a social group, it can be highly instructive (though not conclusive) to observe how people behave in 'abnormal times' – when (*ex hypothesi*) 'submission and intellectual subordination' are absent or diminished, when the apparatus of power is removed or relaxed. Gramsci himself gives the example of 'the fortunes of religions and churches':

[2] Note Gramsci's reliance on the notion of autonomy here.

Religion, or a particular church, maintains its community of faithful (within the limits imposed by the necessities of general historical development) in so far as it nourishes its faith permanently and in an organised fashion, indefatigably repeating its apologetics, struggling at all times and always with the same kind of arguments, and maintaining a hierarchy of intellectuals who give to the faith, in appearance at least, the dignity of thought. Whenever the continuity of relations between the Church and the faithful has been violently interrupted, for political reasons, as happened during the French Revolution, the losses suffered by the Church have been incalculable. (p. 340)

As a contemporary example, consider the reactions of Czechs to the relaxation of the apparatus of power in 1968.

But evidence can also be sought in 'normal times'. We are concerned to find out what the exercise of power prevents people from doing, and sometimes even thinking. Hence we should examine how people react to opportunities – or, more precisely, perceived opportunities – when these occur, to escape from subordinate positions in hierarchical systems. In this connection data about rates of social mobility can acquire a new and striking theoretical significance. The caste system is often thought of as a plausible candidate for 'a case of genuine consensus over different values'. But the whole recent debate over 'Sanskritisation' suggests otherwise. The caste system, according to Srinivas,

is far from a rigid system in which the position of each component caste is fixed for all time. Movement has always been possible, and especially so in the middle regions of the hierarchy. A low caste was able, in a generation or two, to rise to a higher position in the hierarchy by adopting vegetarianism and teetotalism, and by Sanskritizing its ritual and pantheon. In short, it took over, as far as possible, the customs, rites and beliefs of the Brahmins, and the adoption of the Brahminic way of life by a low caste seems to have been frequent, though theoretically forbidden. This process has been called 'Sanskritization'. . . .[3]

[3] M. N. Srinivas, *Religion and Society among the Coorgs of South India* (Oxford: Clarendon Press, 1952) p. 30.

Srinivas argues that 'economic betterment . . . seems to lead to the Sanskritization of the customs and way of life of a group', which itself depends on 'the collective desire to rise high in the esteem of friends, neighbours and rivals' and is followed by 'the adoption of methods by which the status of the group is raised'.[4] Such a desire is, it seems, usually preceded by the acquisition of wealth, but the acquisition of political power, education and leadership also seems to be relevant. In brief, the evidence suggests that there is a significant difference between the caste system as it exists in the 'popular conception' and as it actually operates.[5] What to the outside observer may appear as a value consensus which sanctifies an extreme, elaborately precise and stable hierarchy actually conceals the fact that perceived opportunities of lower castes to rise within the system are very often, if not invariably, seized.

It could be argued that this is not a very persuasive case, since upward mobility within a hierarchical system implies acceptance of the hierarchy, so that the Sanskritising castes are not rejecting but embracing the value system. But against this it can be objected that this is precisely a case of a gap between thought and action, since the adoption of the Brahminic way of life by a low caste is theoretically forbidden and in general caste position is held to be ascriptive, hereditary and unchangeable.

Other, less ambiguous, evidence relating to the Indian caste system can, however, be adduced which supports the claim that the internalisation of subordinate status is a consequence of power. Consider the effects of the introduction of universal suffrage upon lower castes' acceptance of the principle of hierarchy.[6] More tellingly still, consider the 'ways out' taken by the Untouchables, above all that of mass conversion into other religions.[7] At various

[4] M. N. Srinivas, *Caste in Modern India and Other Essays* (London: Asia Publishing House, 1962) pp. 56–7.
[5] Ibid. p. 56.
[6] See, e.g., A. H. Somjee, 'Political Dynamics of a Gujarat Village', *Asian Survey*, 12, 7 (July 1972) pp. 602–8. Somjee writes that in the village he studied, 'In the five successive panchayat elections, respect for age, cohesiveness of caste and kin-group, and familial status gradually declined. The elective principle, which was at the heart of the structural changes, had made serious inroads into the sociopolitical continuum of the traditional society. The all-pervading trends emanating from the old social organization and affecting the structure of community politics and its attitude to authority began to be reversed.' (p. 604)
[7] See Harold R. Isaacs, *India's Ex-Untouchables* (New York: John Day Company, 1964) esp. ch. 12, 'Ways Out'.

periods in their history, the Untouchables have embraced Islam,[8] Christianity and Buddhism,[9] because they proclaimed egalitarian principles and offered the hope of escape from caste discrimination.[10]

I conclude, then, that, in general, evidence can be adduced (though by nature of the case, such evidence will never be conclusive) which supports the relevant counterfactuals implicit in identifying exercises of power of the three-dimensional type. One can take steps to find out what it is that people would have done otherwise.

How, in the second place, is one to identify the process or mechanism of an alleged exercise of power, on the three-dimensional view? (I shall leave aside the further problems of identifying an operative exercise of power, that is, the problem of overdetermination. That is a whole issue in itself.) There are three features, distinctive of the three-dimensional view, which pose peculiarly acute problems for the researcher. As I have argued, such an exercise may in the first place involve inaction rather than (observable) action. In the second place it may be unconscious (this seems to be allowed for on the two-dimensional view, but the latter also insists that nondecisions are *decisions* – and, in the absence of further explanation, an unconscious decision looks like a contradiction). And in the third place power may be exercised by collectivities, such as groups or institutions. Let us examine these difficulties in turn.

First, inaction. Here, once more, we have a non-event. Indeed, where the suppression of a potential issue is attributed to inaction, we have a *double* non-event. How can such a situation be identified empirically? The first step to answering this is to see that

[8] See *The Encyclopedia of Islam*, ed. B. Lewis *et al.*, new edn. (Leiden: Brill, and London: Luzac, 1967) vol. III, pp. 428–9. When the Muslims conquered India's caste cities in the eleventh and twelfth centuries, the result was that 'the egalitarian principles of Islam attracted large numbers of non-caste Hindus and professional groups to the fold of Islam' (ibid.).

[9] The most notable recent instance was the mass conversion of Untouchables to Buddhism under B. R. Ambedkhar's leadership in 1956. In a famous speech in 1936, Ambedkhar had said, 'My self-respect cannot assimilate Hinduism . . . I tell you, religion is for men, not men for religion . . . The religion that does not recognise you as human beings, or give you water to drink, or allow you to enter the temples is not worthy to be called a religion. . . .' (cited in Isaacs, *India's Ex-Untouchables*, p. 173).

[10] Though caste lines were, in fact, maintained within the social systems of the Christians and the Muslims (see Isaacs, ibid. p. 171).

inaction need not be a featureless non-event. The failure to act in a certain way, in a given situation, may well have specifiable consequences, where acting in that way is a hypothesised possibility with determinate consequences. Moreover, the consequence of inaction may well be a further non-event, such as the non-appearance of a political issue, where the actions in question would, *ex hypothesi*, have led to its appearance. There seems to be no impossibility in principle of establishing a causal nexus here : the relation between the inaction of U.S. Steel and the public silence over air pollution is an admirable case in point.

Second, unconsciousness. How can power be exercised without the exerciser being aware of what he (it) is doing? Here it will be useful to make a number of distinctions (and, for brevity, in what follows I use the term 'action' to cover the case of inaction). There are a number of ways of being unconscious of what one is doing. One may be unaware of what is held to be the 'real' motive or meaning of one's action (as in standard Freudian cases). Or, second, one may be unaware of how others interpret one's action. Or, third, one may be unaware of the consequences of one's action. Identifying an unconscious exercise of power of the first type presents the usual difficulty, characteristic of Freudian-type explanations, of establishing the 'real' motive or meaning, where the interpretations of observer and observed differ. This difficulty, however, is well-known and has been very widely discussed, and it is not peculiar to the analysis of power. Identifying an unconscious exercise of power of the second type seems to pose no particular problem. It is the third type which is really problematic, in cases where the agent *could not be expected* to have knowledge of the consequences of his action. Can A properly be said to exercise power over B where knowledge of the effects of A upon B is just not available to A? If A's ignorance of those effects is due to his (remediable) failure to find out, the answer appears to be yes. Where, however, he could not have found out – because, say, certain factual or technical knowledge was simply not *available* – then talk of an exercise of power appears to lose all its point. Consider, for instance, the case of a drug company which allegedly exercises the most extreme power – of life and death – over members of the public by marketing a dangerous drug. Here the allegation that power is being exercised is not refuted if it could be shown that the company's scientists and managers did not know that the drug's effects were dangerous: they could have taken steps to find out. On the other hand, did cigarette companies exercise this power over the public before it was even supposed that cigarette smoking might be harmful? Surely not. This suggests that where power is held to be exercised unconsciously in this sense (i.e. in unawareness of its consequences), the assumption is being made that the exerciser or exercisers could, in the context, have ascertained those consequences. (Of course, justifying that assumption raises further problems, since it involves, for example, the making of historical judgments about the locus of culturally determined limits to cognitive innovation.)

The third difficulty is that of attributing an exercise of power to collectivities, such as groups, classes or institutions. The problem is: when can social causation be characterised as an exercise of power, or, more precisely, how and where is the line to be drawn between structural determination, on the one hand, and an exercise of power, on the other? This is a problem which has often reappeared in the history of Marxist thought, in the context of discussions of determinism and voluntarism. Thus, for example, within post-war French Marxism, an extreme determinist position is adopted by the structuralist Marxism of Louis Althusser and his followers, as opposed to the so-called 'humanist', 'historicist' and 'subjectivist' interpretations of thinkers such as Sartre and Lucien Goldmann, and behind them of Lukàcs and Korsch (and, behind them, of Hegel) for whom the historical 'subject' has a crucial and ineradicable explanatory role. For Althusser, Marx's thought, properly understood, conceptualises 'the determination of the elements of a whole by the structure of the whole', and 'liberated definitively from the empiricist antinomies of phenomenal subjectivity and essential interiority', treats of 'an objective system governed, in its most concrete determinations, by the laws of its *arrangement* (*montage*) and of its *machinery*, by the specifications of its concept'.[11]

The implications of this position can be seen very clearly in the debate between the Althusserian, Nicos Poulantzas, and

[11] L. Althusser and E. Balibar, *Lire Le Capital* (Paris: Maspero, 1968) vol. 11, pp. 63, 71.

the British political sociologist, Ralph Miliband, over the latter's book *The State in Capitalist Society* [21]. According to Poulantzas, Miliband had

> difficulties . . . in comprehending social classes and the State as *objective structures*, and their relations as an *objective system of regular connections*, a structure and a system whose agents, 'men', are in the words of Marx, 'bearers' of it – *träger*. Miliband constantly gives the impression that for him social classes or 'groups' are in some way reducible to *inter-personal relations*, that the State is reducible to inter-personal relations of the members of the diverse 'groups' that constitute the State apparatus, and finally that the relation between social classes and the State is itself reducible to inter-personal relations of 'individuals' composing social groups and 'individuals' composing the State apparatus. ([32] p. 70)

This conception, Poulantzas continues

> seems to me to derive from a *problematic of the subject* which has had constant repercussions in the history of Marxist thought. According to this problematic, the agents of a social formation, 'men', are not considered as the 'bearers' of objective instances (as they are for Marx), but as the genetic principle of the levels of the social whole. This is a problematic of *social actors*, of individuals as the origin of *social action* : sociological research thus leads finally, not to the study of the objective co-ordinates that determine the distribution of agents into social classes and the contradictions between these classes, but to the search for *finalist* explanations founded on the *motivations of conduct* of the individual actors. (p. 70)

Miliband, in response to this, maintains that Poulantzas

> is here rather one-sided and that he goes much too far in dismissing the nature of the state elite as of altogether no account. For what his *exclusive* stress on 'objective relations' suggests is that what the state does is in every particular and at all times *wholly* determined by these 'objective relations' : in other words, that the structural constraints of the system are so absolutely compelling as to turn those who run the state into the

53

merest functionaries and executants of policies imposed upon them by 'the system'. ([22] p. 57)

Poulantzas, writes Miliband, substitutes 'the notion of "objective structures" and "objective relations" for the notion of a "ruling" class', and his analysis leads 'straight towards a kind of structural determinism, or rather a structural super-determinism, which makes impossible a truly realistic consideration of the dialectical relationship between the State and "the system" ' (p. 57).[12]

The first thing to say about this debate is that Poulantzas's implied dichotomy between structural determinism and methodological individualism – between his own 'problematic' and that of 'social actors, of individuals as the origin of social action' – is misleading. These are not the only two possibilities. It is not a question of sociological research 'leading finally' *either* to the study of 'objective co-ordinates' *or* to that of 'motivations of conduct of the individual actors'. Such research must clearly examine the complex interrelations between the two, and allow for the obvious fact that individuals act together and upon one another within groups and organisations, and that the explanation of their behaviour and interaction is unlikely to be reducible merely to their individual motivations.

The second thing to say about the Poulantzas–Miliband debate is that it turns on a crucially important conceptual distinction – which the language of power serves to mark out. To use the vocabulary of power in the context of social relationships is to speak of human agents, separately or together, in groups or organisations, through action or inaction, significantly affecting the thoughts or actions of others (specifically, in a manner contrary to their interests). In speaking thus, one assumes that, although the agents operate within structurally determined limits, they none the less have a certain relative autonomy and could have acted differently. The future, though it is not entirely open, is not entirely closed either (and, indeed, the degree of its openness is itself structurally determined).[13] In short, within a system character-

[12] The Poulantzas–Miliband debate is reproduced in Urry and Wakeford [35]. It is discussed by Ernest Laclau in *Economy and Society* (Feb 1975) and continued by Poulantzas in *New Left Review*, no. 95 (1976).

[13] Compare Wright Mills:
Fate is a feature of specific kinds of social structure; the extent to which the mechanics of fate are the mechanics of history-making is itself a historical problem. . . .

ised by total structural determinism, there would be no place for power.

Of course, one always has the alternative of stipulatively re-defining 'power' in terms of structural determination. This is the path which Poulantzas takes in his book *Political Power and Social Classes* [33]. He defines his concept of power as '*the capacity of a social class to realize its specific objective interests*' (p. 104) and argues that this concept '*points to the effects of the structure on the relations of conflict between the practices of the various classes in "struggle"*. In other words, power is not located in the levels of structures, but is an effect of the ensemble of these levels . . .' (p. 99). Class relations are '*at every level relations of power*: power, however, is only a concept indicating the effect of the ensemble of the structures on *the relations of the practices of the various classes in conflict*' (p. 101). But this conceptual assimilation of power to structural determination simply serves to obscure a crucial distinction which it is theoretically necessary to make, and which the vocabulary of power articulates. My claim, in other words, is that to identify a given process as an 'exercise of power', rather than as a case of structural determination, is to assume that it is *in the exerciser's or exercisers' power* to act differently. In the case of a collective exercise of power, or the part of a group, or institution, etc., this is to imply that the members of the group or institution could have combined or organised to act differently.

The justification of this claim, and the key to the latter two difficulties involved in the identification of the process of exercising power, lies in the relation between power and responsibility.[14] The reason why identifying such an exercise involves the assump-

In those societies in which the means of power are involuntary and de-centralized, history *is* fate. The innumerable actions of innumerable men modify their local milieus, and thus gradually modify the structure of society as a whole. These modifications – the course of history – go on behind men's backs. History is drift, although in total 'men make it'.

But in those societies in which the means of power are enormous in scope and centralized in form a few men may be so placed within the historical structure that by their decisions about the use of these means they modify the structural conditions under which most men live. Nowadays such elites of power make history, 'under circumstances not chosen altogether by themselves', yet compared with other men, and with other periods of human history, these circumstances do indeed seem less overwhelming. . . . [24] pp. 21–2).

[14] On this point, see William Connolly's excellent discussion of power in his forthcoming book, *The Terms of Political Discourse* (Boston: D. C. Heath).

tion that the exerciser(s) could have acted differently – and, where they are unaware of the consequences of their action or inaction, that they could have ascertained these – is that an attribution of power is at the same time an attribution of (partial or total) responsibility for certain consequences. The point, in other words, of locating power is to fix responsibility for consequences held to flow from the action, or inaction, of certain specifiable agents. We cannot here enter into a discussion of the notion of responsibility (and the problems of identifying collective responsibility): it is no less problematic – and essentially contested – a notion than the others examined in this essay. Nor can we here discuss the underlying theoretical (and non-empirical?) issue of how one determines where structural determination ends and power and responsibility begin. But it is worth noting, in conclusion, that C. Wright Mills perceived the relations I have argued for between these concepts in his distinction between *fate* and power. His 'sociological conception of fate' had, he wrote, 'to do with events in history that are beyond the control of any circle or groups of men (1) compact enough to be identifiable, (2) powerful enough to decide with consequence, and (3) in a position to foresee the consequences and so to be held accountable for historical events' ([24] p. 21).[15] He argued in favour of attributing power to those in strategic positions who are able to initiate changes that are in the interests of broad segments of society but do not, claiming it to be 'now sociologically realistic, morally fair, and politically imperative to make demands upon men of power and to hold them responsible for specific courses of events' (p. 100).

[15] Cited in Connolly, *The Terms of Political Discourse.*

9. CONCLUSION

THE one-dimensional view of power offers a clear-cut paradigm for the behavioural study of decision-making power by political actors, but it inevitably takes over the bias of the political system under observation and is blind to the ways in which its political agenda is controlled. The two-dimensional view points the way to examining that bias and control, but conceives of them too narrowly: in a word, it lacks a sociological perspective within which to examine, not only decision-making and non-decision-making power, but also the various ways of suppressing latent conflicts within society. Such an examination poses a number of serious difficulties.

These difficulties are serious but not overwhelming.[1] They certainly do not require us to consign the three-dimensional view of power to the realm of the merely metaphysical or the merely ideological. My conclusion, in short, is that a deeper analysis of power relations is possible – an analysis that is at once value-laden, theoretical and empirical.[2] A pessimistic attitude towards the possibility of such an analysis is unjustified. As Frey has written ([14] p. 1095), such pessimism amounts to saying: 'Why let things be difficult when, with just a little more effort, we can make them seem impossible?'

---

[1] These are pressed further by Alan Bradshaw in his 'A Critique of Steven Lukes' *Power: A Radical View*', *Sociology*, 10 (1976) pp. 121–7, and re-examined by the present author in his 'Reply to Bradshaw', ibid. pp. 129–32.

[2] For a fine example of such an analysis, see J. P. Gaventa, 'Power and Powerlessness: Quiescence and Rebellion in an Appalachian Valley', thesis presented for degree of Doctor of Philosophy, deposited at Bodleian Library, Oxford.

BIBLIOGRAPHY

[1] Hannah Arendt, *On Violence* (London: Allen Lane, The Penguin Press, 1970). A characteristically stimulating essay, advancing an interestingly idiosyncratic concept of power.

[2] Peter Bachrach and Morton S. Baratz, 'The Two Faces of Power', *American Political Science Review*, 56 (1962) pp. 947–52. A brilliant and by now classical contribution to the literature.

[3] ——, 'Decisions and Nondecisions: An Analytical Framework', *American Political Science Review*, 57 (1963) pp. 641–51. A crucial further development of the above.

[4] ——, *Power and Poverty. Theory and Practice* (New York: Oxford University Press, 1970). The first, theoretical part incorporates and develops the two foregoing items (toning down the potentially three-dimensional implications of the second); the second part is an empirical study of the politics of poverty and race relations in Baltimore.

[5] Isaac D. Balbus, 'The Concept of Interest in Pluralist and Marxian Analysis', *Politics and Society*, 1 (1971) pp. 151–77. Relates the subjective definition of 'interest' used by pluralists to classical liberalism and argues for the explanatory and normative superiority of Marxian class analysis.

[6] Samuel Beer, *Modern British Politics* (London: Faber, 1965). Gives an alternative, two-dimensional account of power in the British Labour Party to that of McKenzie [19], stressing power over the agenda of party pol

[7] Roderick Bell, David V. Edwards and R. Harrison Wagner (eds), *Political Power: A Reader in Theory and Research* (New York: The Free Press; London: Collier-Macmillan, 1969). A very useful collection, reprinting, *inter alia*, Bachrach and Baratz [2, 3], Dahl [10, 11], part of Polsby [30] and Parsons [28].

[8] William E. Connolly, 'On "Interests" in Politics', *Politics and Society*, 2 (1972) pp. 459–77. A valuable discussion of alternative efforts to elucidate the descriptive criteria of 'interests', including a thought-provoking account of 'real interests'.

[9] Matthew A. Crenson, *The Un-Politics of Air Pollution: A Study of Non-Decisionmaking in the Cities* (Baltimore and London: The Johns Hopkins Press, 1971). A very intelligent and ingenious empirical application of the two-dimensional view of power, together with certain elements of the three-dimensional view.

[10] Robert A. Dahl, 'The Concept of Power', *Behavioral Science*, 2 (1957) pp. 201–5. Dahl's first, rather crude effort to define and operationalise 'power'.

[11] ——, 'A Critique of the Ruling Elite Model', *American Political Science Review*, 52 (1958) pp. 463–9. Argues that the ruling elite hypothesis can be strictly tested only if the alleged elite is 'well defined' and has preferences which regularly prevail over opposition in key political decisions.

[12] ——, *Who Governs? Democracy and Power in an American City* (New Haven and London: Yale University Press, 1961). The classical 'pluralist' study. A finer, subtler work than its critics and defenders might suggest, partly because it contains the evidential basis for criticising its conclusions.

[13] Ralf Dahrendorf, *Class and Class Conflict in Industrial Society* (London: Routledge & Kegan Paul, 1959). Offers a 'coercion theory of social structure' and focuses on authority relations in imperatively co-ordinated associations where there are antagonistic socially structured 'objective' interests.

[14] Frederic W. Frey, 'Comment: On Issues and Nonissues

in the Study of Power', *American Political Science Review*, 65 (1971) pp. 1081–101. A careful, probing article (in reply to Wolfinger [37]) which argues for the researchability of nonissues.

[15] W. B. Gallie, 'Essentially Contested Concepts', *Proceedings of the Aristotelian Society*, 56 (1955–6) pp. 167–98. Expounds the idea of there being concepts whose application is inherently a matter of dispute.

[16] Anthony Giddens, ' "Power" in the Recent Writings of Talcott Parsons', *Sociology*, 2 (1968) pp. 257–72. An incisive critique of Parsons [26, 27, 28] for simply setting aside or ignoring the main points at issue between integration and coercion theory.

[17] Antonio Gramsci, *Selections from the Prison Notebooks of Antonio Gramsci*, ed. and trans. Quintin Hoare and Geoffrey Nowell-Smith (London: Lawrence & Wishart, 1971). A full selection of Gramsci's writings on history, politics and philosophy, including his thoughts on the exercise of power by means of ideological 'hegemony'.

[18] Lewis Lipsitz, 'On Political Belief: The Grievances of the Poor', in *Power and Community: Dissenting Essays in Political Science*, ed. Philip Green and Sanford Levinson (New York: Random House, Vintage Books, 1970). A subtle discussion of 'political silence', focusing on unarticulated and latent grievances.

[19] R. T. McKenzie, *British Political Parties: The Distribution of Power within the Conservative and Labour Parties*, 2nd rev. edn. with new chapter on events since 1955 (London: Heinemann, Mercury Books edition, 1964). Argues, on the basis of the one-dimensional view, that 'the distribution of power within the two major parties is the same' (p. 635) – namely, pyramidal.

[20] Richard M. Merelman, 'On the Neo-Elitist Critique of Community Power', *American Political Science Review*, 62 (1968) pp. 451–50. A lively attack on the idea of non-decision-making and 'the false consensus argument' and a defence of a decisional methodology and pluralist premises.

[21] Ralph Miliband, *The State in Capitalist Society* (London:

Weidenfeld & Nicolson, 1969). A study of 'the vast inflation of the state's power and activity in the advanced capitalist societies' (p. 1), including an analysis of various agencies of legitimation, such as parties, the mass media and education.

[22] ——, 'The Capitalist State: Reply to Nicos Poulantzas', *New Left Review*, 59 (Jan–Feb 1970) pp. 53–60. Spirited reply to Poulantzas [32] which accuses him of 'structural super-determinism' and argues that 'the state elite is involved in a far more complex relationship with "the system" and with society as a whole than Poulantzas's scheme allows' (p. 57).

[23] ——, Review of Poulantzas [34], *New Left Review*, 82 (Nov–Dec 1973) pp. 83–92.

[24] C. Wright Mills, *The Causes of World War Three* (London: Secker & Warburg, 1959). Contains some provocative thoughts on the (historically relative and structurally determined) distinction between 'fate' and power and on the relation between power and responsibility.

[25] Peter Morriss, 'Power in New Haven: A Reassessment of "Who Governs?" ', *British Journal of Political Science*, 2 (1972) pp. 457–65. A useful discussion of Dahl [12].

[26] Talcott Parsons, 'The Distribution of Power in American Society', *World Politics*, 10 (Oct 1957) pp. 123–43. A review article of C. Wright Mills's, *The Power Elite* (New York: Oxford University Press, 1956), in which Parsons first elaborated his consensual concept of power and criticised the 'zero sum' concept as 'misleading and one-sided'.

[27] ——, 'On the Concept of Influence', *Public Opinion Quarterly*, 27 (1963) pp. 37–62.

[28] ——, 'On the Concept of Political Power', *Proceedings of the American Philosophical Society*, 107 (1963) pp. 232–62. The two fullest elaborations of Parsons's later view of power.

[29] ——, *Sociological Theory and Modern Society* (New York: The Free Press; London: Collier-Macmillan, 1967). Reproduces Parsons [27, 28] as well as other relevant essays.

[30] Nelson W. Polsby, *Community Power and Political Theory* (New Haven and London: Yale University Press, 1963). An examination of the community power literature which attacks 'stratification writers' and defends a decisional methodology, testable theory and pluralist conclusions.

[31] ——, 'COMMUNITY: The Study of Community Power', *International Encyclopaedia of the Social Sciences*, vol. 3 (New York: Macmillan and Free Press, 1968) pp. 157–63. A survey of methods, findings and interpretations which mentions but does not acknowledge the force of the critical point that 'an ongoing political system can be regarded as a stacked deck of cards' (p. 161).

[32] Nicos Poulantzas, 'The Problem of the Capitalist State', *New Left Review*, 58 (Nov–Dec 1969) pp. 67–78. A critique of Miliband [21], accusing it, *inter alia*, of being 'unduly influenced by the methodological principles of the adversary' (p. 70) in focusing on social actors rather than on objective structures.

[33] ——, *Political Power and Social Classes*, translation ed. Timothy O'Hagan (London: N.L.B. and Sheed & Ward, 1973). An abstract and conceptual analysis, *à la* Althusser, of the position and function of the State under capitalism, which dissolves 'power' into a form of structural determinism.

[34] E. E. Schattschneider, *The Semi-Sovereign People: A Realist's View of Democracy in America* (New York: Holt, Rinehart & Winston, 1960). The *locus classicus* for the notion of the 'mobilisation of bias'.

[35] John Urry and John Wakeford (eds), *Power in Britain: Sociological Readings* (London: Heinemann Educational Books, 1973). A useful collection of articles, empirical and theoretical, including the Poulantzas–Miliband debate.

[36] D. M. White, 'The Problems of Power', *British Journal of Political Science*, 2 (1972) pp. 479–90. A useful, clarifying discussion which argues against the possibility of a universally satisfactory account of the meaning of 'power' and analyses it as a form of significant affecting.

[37] Raymond E. Wolfinger, 'Nondecisions and the Study of Local Politics', *American Political Science Review*, 65 (1971) pp. 1063–80. A rather diffuse defence of decisionism and pluralism and a further attack on the study of non-decision-making, concluding with scepticism about the possibility of investigating 'power structures' at all.

[38] ——, 'Rejoinder to Frey's "Comment" ', *American Political Science Review*, 65 (1971) pp. 1102–4. A one-dimensional response to a two-dimensional critique.